The Wright Brothers' FIRST FLIGHT

A FLY on the WALL HISTORY

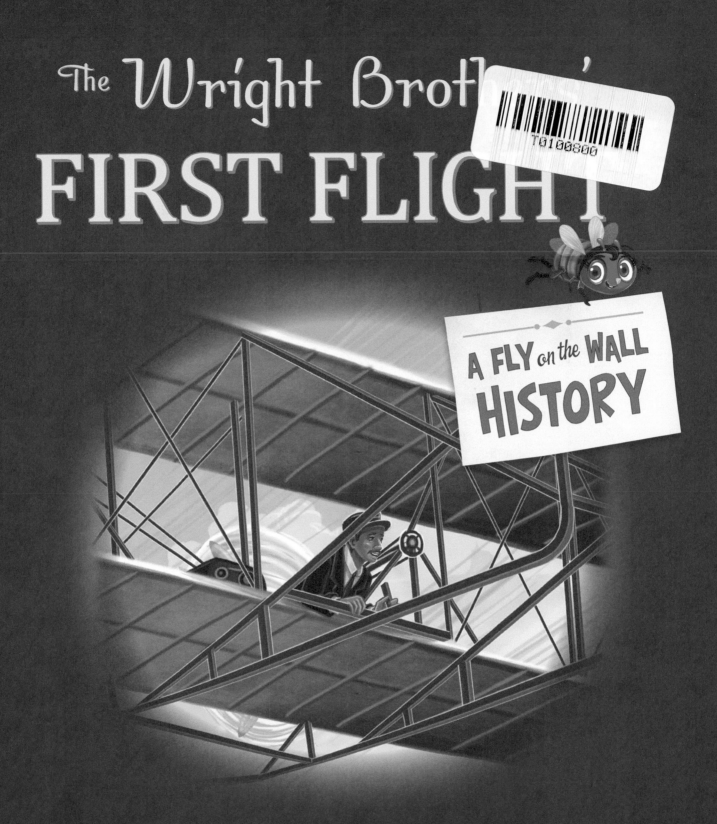

BY THOMAS KINGSLEY TROUPE   ILLUSTRATED BY JOMIKE TEJIDO

PICTURE WINDOW BOOKS
a capstone imprint

Hi, I'm Maggie, and this is my brother, Horace.

We've been "flies on the wall" during important events in history.

We watched Leonardo da Vinci paint the famous *Mona Lisa*.

We even rode with Rosa Parks on a bus.

We sailed with the Pilgrims on the *Mayflower*.

Another high-flying adventure started when we found two brothers who wanted to fly ... like us!

2

One day in 1903, Horace and I found ourselves in Dayton, Ohio. We were outside a bicycle shop, listening to two men talking. The men were brothers named Orville and Wilbur Wright. They wanted a way for people to travel through the air. Ha! Funny stuff. People can't fly! Only bugs and birds can do that.

We've seen humans try to fly before, haven't we, Maggie?

Yep. It always ends in a crash or someone getting hurt.

3

Horace and I were curious, so we flew into the shop to hear more. We saw drawings of wings the brothers were going to build. The wings didn't look anything like the ones on our backs.

★ ★ ★

The Wright brothers also owned a printing shop.
Skills from both businesses helped them design and build their airplanes.

★ ★ ★

The Wright brothers called their fake wings a flying machine.
They worked on it when they weren't fixing bikes.

The Wrights already build bicycles. And people love them!

Isn't that enough?

Guess not! They still want to fly.

These guys don't like to sit still.

I saw a photo of Wilbur ... and he was flying! He was lying down on something the brothers called their 1902 glider. They talked about how they wanted to be able to go farther.

The 1902 glider was the third glider the Wright brothers had built. They connected bicycle chains to a small moving flap called an elevator. Pulling the chains made the glider go up or down. The brothers steered by moving their hips.

So, they can sort of fly, right?
Doesn't gliding count as flying?

I'm not sure.

I think they want to be able to fly longer and farther.

Like we do, Horace!

★ ★ ★

The 1902 glider was much better than the first two gliders. The pilot could shift his hips to "warp the wings." This allowed the glider to turn.

★ ★ ★   7

Horace and I stuck around a while.
Orville and Wilbur talked about
building an engine for their flying
machine. They got help from a man
named Charles Taylor.

"The engine has to be lightweight,"
Orville said. "No more than
200 pounds [91 kilograms]."

"We need it to produce at least
8 horsepower," Wilbur said.

Horsepower?

They're going to power
their flying machine
with HORSES?!

Awesome!

No, Horace. That's
how powerful the
engine will be—eight
horses' worth.

The engine the Wright brothers built was made mostly of aluminum and a little bit of copper.
In 1903, aluminum was one of the lightest metals around.

The Wright brothers were really smart. They weren't messing around. They worked with a wooden box with a fan attached to it. It was called a wind tunnel. They used it to test wings for their new flyer. I flew by the wind tunnel once for a closer look. It blew me away!

* * *

The Wright brothers had fun names for their wind tunnel openings. The end where the fan blew air in was called the "goesinta." The end where the air escaped was called "goesouta."

* * *

Next, Orville and Wilbur carved long sticks called propellers.
They planned to attach them to the engine using bicycle chains.

They're going to hang
little model flyers
inside the wind tunnel.

That's a good way
to test the design
before making
a full-size flyer.

Yeah. If I didn't already
have wings, I'd pilot one of
those mini flyers!

Could this flying machine work? We were going to find out! Horace and I followed the brothers to a place called Kitty Hawk, North Carolina. Horace was spooked at first. He's afraid of hawks. Kitty Hawk had a lot of sand dunes, hills, and wind. But I didn't see any hawks.

Will the hawks get mad at the Wright brothers for flying around?

You know how I feel about hawks, Maggie.

I don't think the brothers have anything to worry about.

People can't fly, remember?

★ ★ ★

The town of Kitty Hawk is located on the Outer Banks. This string of islands sits off the eastern coast of North Carolina.

★ ★ ★

Orville and Wilbur unpacked the flyer pieces in a big empty building. They called it a hangar. I guess that's where the flyer was going to "hang out" once they put it together.

The Wright brothers put on the wings first. Next they put the propellers and engine into place. Orville looked worried. He told Wilbur their flyer might be too heavy.

I'm just a little fly, but I'm a HUGE expert on flying. The brothers' flyer was 21 feet (6.4 meters) long. And the whole thing weighed 605 pounds (274 kilograms). There was no way that thing was going to fly.

I can't believe
they're still going
to try.

Those guys are
going to be so
bummed.

It's a cool-looking flyer.
But I worry that it's
going to break.

Or that they'll break
their necks!

★ ★ ★

The engine built for the 1903 flyer was 12 horsepower. The brothers hoped
the more powerful engine would keep the heavier flyer in the air.

★ ★ ★

15

With the weather just right, it was time to try and fly. A group of men pushed the flyer up the hill. The brothers said a prayer, and Wilbur took out a coin. He flipped it to see who would try the flyer first. Wilbur won.

16

The engine started, and boy, was it loud! Two kids and a dog got scared and ran away. The flyer slid on the rail and started to lift. A few seconds later, the engine stopped, and the flyer crashed.

Maggie, am I wrong, or did it look like the flyer sort of ... flew?

Sort of, but not for very long.

The Wrights didn't think that counted as flying.

★ ★ ★

The 1903 flyer's first try resulted in a flight of 3.5 seconds and a distance of 18 inches (46 centimeters).

★ ★ ★

17

The Wright brothers weren't going to give up. They worked quickly to repair the damage. Wilbur sent a telegram to their dad, Bishop Milton Wright. He wanted him to know how things were going.

THE WESTERN UNION TELEGRAPH COMPANY.

Form No. 168.

INCORPORATED

23,000 OFFICES IN AMERICA. CABLE SERVICE TO ALL THE WORLD.

This Company TRANSMITS and DELIVERS messages only o...conditions limiting its liability, which have been assented to by the sender of the following message.
Errors can be guarded against only by repeating a message back to the sending station for comparison, and the Company will not hold itself liable for errors or delays
in transmission or delivery of Unrepeated Messages, beyond the amount of tolls paid thereon, nor in any case where the claim is not presented in writing within sixty days
after the message is filed with the Company for transmission.
This is an UNREPEATED MESSAGE, and is delivered by request of the sender, under the conditions named above.
ROBERT C. CLOWRY, President and General Manager.

RECEIVED at

176 C KA GS 33 Paid.   Via Norfolk Va

Kitty Hawk N C Dec 15

Bishop M Wright

7 Hawthorne St

There is now no question of final success   rudder

only injured   success assured   keep quiet

* * *

While repairing the flyer's rudder, the weather
was perfect. When the repairs were complete, the
weather was not so perfect. The Wright brothers
had to wait one more day to try again.

* * *

So the flyer is
ready to go, but now
there's no wind?

That stinks!

It does.

But these guys are
NOT going to quit.

Maybe tomorrow?

19

Morning came, and I nudged Horace awake. He said he had been dreaming about flies riding bicycles ...

Everyone was ready to watch the Wright brothers' second try. There was even a man with a camera. We buzzed over to watch.

This time it was Orville's turn to be the pilot. He climbed aboard. The engine started, and the flyer moved down the rail. I was pretty sure it was going to crash again. But it didn't. The flyer actually flew! It didn't stay up for long, but it flew!

* * *

The 1903 flyer stayed in the air for 12 seconds.
It flew 120 feet (37 m) away from the rail.
The flyer's maximum height was 20 feet (6.1 m).

* * *

The brothers' short first flight wasn't enough. Horace and I watched them try again and again. They took turns. Each time the flyer flew a little farther and a little longer.

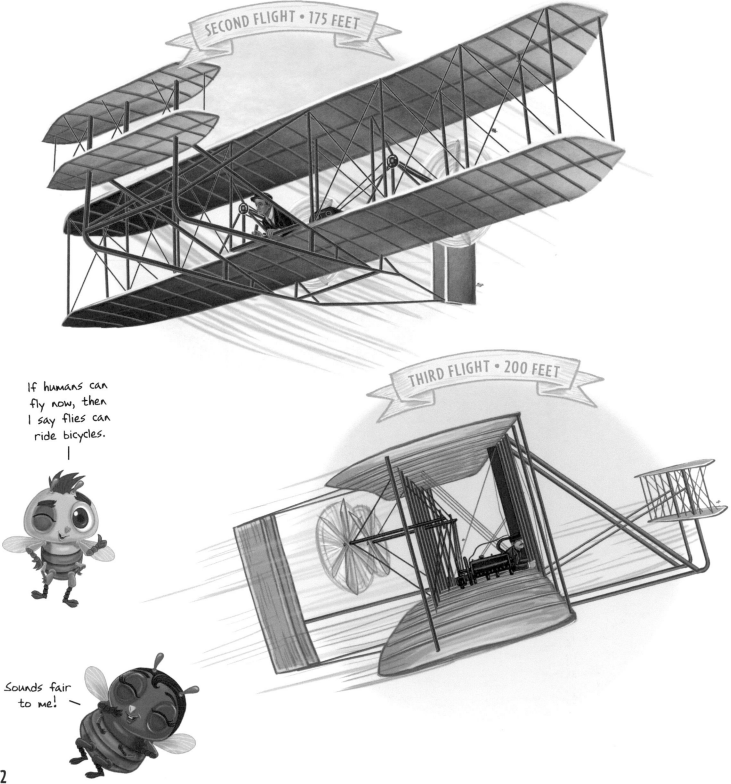

SECOND FLIGHT • 175 FEET

THIRD FLIGHT • 200 FEET

If humans can fly now, then I say flies can ride bicycles.

Sounds fair to me!

Wilbur flew for the fourth and final time that day. The flyer was in the air for almost a minute. It flew 852 feet (260 m)! The Wright brothers had done it. They had invented the first working airplane!

* * *

Other inventors were trying to be the first to fly. The most notable was Charles Langley. His aircraft, the Aerodrome, failed. It crashed into the Potomac River weeks before the Wright brothers' first flight.

* * *

Horace and I stuck around. We wanted to see Orville and Wilbur fly some more the next day. If they flew farther each time, who knew how far they could go? But that wasn't going to happen.

Without warning, a gust of wind blew across the dunes. It caught the flyer and flipped it over, knocking it to pieces. No one was hurt, but the world's first airplane was never going to fly again. Even so, the Wright brothers didn't seem too upset. They knew how to fly. Any new machine they built would be even better.

I'm glad they flew a few times before the flyer was destroyed.

This reminds me of that time I got whacked by a ceiling fan! Super ouch!

Ha! I remember that. You were dizzy for a week!

The Wright brothers packed up the pieces to the 1903 flyer and shipped them back to Dayton. The pieces stayed in crates for 13 years.

✦ ✦ ✦

Even though their flyer was wrecked, the Wright brothers felt good. They wanted to share their news with their family back home. They sent a telegram.

THE WESTERN UNION TELEGRAPH COMPANY.
INCORPORATED
23,000 OFFICES IN AMERICA.   CABLE SERVICE TO ALL THE WORLD.

Form No. 168.

This Company TRANSMITS and DELIVERS messages only o . conditions limiting its liability, which have been assented to by the sender of the following message.
Errors can be guarded against only by repeating a message back to the sending station for comparison, and the Company will not hold itself liable for errors or delays
in transmission or delivery of Unrepeated Messages, beyond the amount of tolls paid thereon, nor in any case where the claim is not presented in writing within sixty days
after the message is filed with the Company for transmission.
This is an UNREPEATED MESSAGE, and is delivered by request of the sender, under the conditions named above.
ROBERT C. CLOWRY, President and General Manager.

RECEIVED at   Via Norfolk Va

176 C KA CS 33 Paid.

Kitty Hawk N C Dec 17

Bishop M Wright

        7 Hawthorne St

Success four flights thursday morning all against twenty one mile
wind started from Level with engine power alone average speed
through air thirty one miles longest 57 seconds inform Press
home christmas .

                              Orevelle Wright   525P

* * *

The telegram sent home had a few mistakes in it.
The longest flight was actually 59 seconds, and Orville's name was spelled wrong.

* * *

I bet they're going
to keep building
flying machines,
aren't they?

Yep. I have a feeling
the skies will be
pretty crowded
soon enough.

The Wright brothers continued to work on their airplanes. The 1903 flyer could fly only in a straight line and for only around one minute. Orville and Wilbur spent two years making new flyers. They made fixes to the controls, engine, and propellers. Near the end of 1905, their new flyer could fly for more than 30 minutes and do figure 8s in the sky.

On October 5, 1905, Wilbur flew 24 miles (39 kilometers) in almost 40 minutes. Four days later, the Wright brothers wrote a letter to the U.S. War Department. They asked if the government would like to buy the world's first practical airplane.

TIMELINE

APRIL 16, 1867
Wilbur Wright is born.

AUGUST 19, 1871
Orville Wright is born.

1893
The Wright Cycle Company opens.

1878
Bishop Milton Wright, father of the Wright brothers, brings home a rubber band-powered toy helicopter. Orville later says the toy gave him and his brother the idea to someday invent a flying machine.

1900
The Wright brothers build a camp in Kitty Hawk, North Carolina. They begin experimenting with kites and gliders.

JULY 1901
The 1901 glider flies nearly 400 feet (122 m).

SEPTEMBER 19 THROUGH OCTOBER 24, 1902
The 1902 glider makes between 700 and 1,000 flights. The farthest it travels is 622.5 feet (190 m).

DECEMBER 14, 1903
Wilbur makes the first unsuccessful attempt to fly the 1903 flyer.

DECEMBER 17, 1903
Orville makes the first "official" manned flight.

JUNE 17 AND 18, 1909
The town of Dayton, Ohio, celebrates the work of the Wright brothers.

MAY THROUGH DECEMBER 1904
The Wrights practice with their new machine. Their longest flight of the year is 5 minutes and 4 seconds, covering a distance of 2.75 miles (4.4 km).

GLOSSARY

carve–to shape by cutting away material such as wood or stone

dune–a hill or ridge of sand piled up by the wind

engineer–a person who uses science and math to plan, design, or build

glider–a lightweight aircraft that flies by floating and rising on air currents instead of by engine power

hangar–a large building in which aircraft are kept

horsepower–a unit for measuring an engine's power

inspire–to influence and encourage someone to do something

propeller–a rotating blade that moves a vehicle through water or air

rudder–a metal plate attached to a plane to help the pilot steer

telegram–a message sent by telegraph, a machine that uses electrical signals to send messages over long distances

THINK ABOUT IT

1. Explain why Kitty Hawk, North Carolina, was a good place for the Wright Brothers to test their new flyer. (Key Ideas and Details)

2. Great inventors are curious. They ask a lot of questions. What other qualities do you think great inventors need to have? Did the Wright Brothers have those qualities? Give examples to support your answer. (Integration of Knowledge and Ideas)

3. What is the main difference between a glider and a flyer? (Craft and Structure)

READ MORE

The Big Book of Airplanes. New York: DK Publishing, 2016.

Nahum, Andrew. *Flight.* DK Eyewitness Books. New York: DK Publishing, 2011.

Stark, William N. *Mighty Military Aircraft.* Military Machines on Duty. North Mankato, Minn.: Capstone Press, a Capstone Imprint, 2016.

INTERNET SITES

FactHound offers a safe, fun way to find Internet sites related to this book. All of the sites on FactHound have been researched by our staff.

Here's all you do:
Visit *www.facthound.com*
Type in this code: 9781479597871

Super-cool stuff!

Check out projects, games and lots more at
www.capstonekids.com

INDEX

Look for all the books in the series:

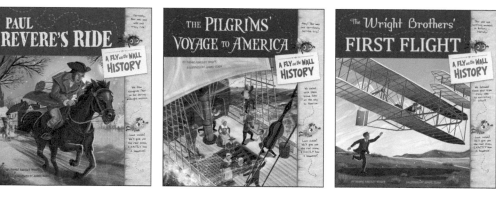

Special thanks to our adviser, Kevin Byrne, PhD, Professor Emeritus of History, Gustavus Adolphus College, for his expertise.

Picture Window Books is published by Capstone,
1710 Roe Crest Drive, North Mankato, Minnesota 56003
www.mycapstone.com

Library of Congress Cataloging-in-Publication data is available on the Library of Congress website.
978-1-4795-9787-1 (library binding)
978-1-4795-9791-8 (paperback)
978-1-4795-9795-6 (eBook PDF)

Summary: Describes the events leading up to and including the historic first flight of aviation pioneers the Wright Brothers in Kitty Hawk, North Carolina, as seen through the eyes of two fictional flies.

Editor: Jill Kalz
Designer: Sarah Bennett
Creative Director: Nathan Gassman
Production Specialist: Steve Walker

The illustrations in this book were planned with pencil on paper and finished with digital paints.

Printed in the United States   5960